THIS WALKER BOOK BELONGS TO:

_____

_____

_____

_____

For thousands of years,
fishermen have watched every autumn
as adult eels migrated down rivers into the sea,
and again every spring as the young eels returned.
But nobody knew what happened in between.
Where did the adults go to?
And where were the young eels born?
Today we think we know the secret of the eel,
but even now no one has ever seen a wild
eel lay eggs or an eel egg hatch.

For Martin Llewellyn
K.W.

For my Dad
M.B.

First published 1993
by Walker Books Ltd
87 Vauxhall Walk
London SE11 5HJ

This edition published 1995

10 9 8 7 6 5 4 3 2 1

Printed in Hong Kong

British Library Cataloguing
in Publication Data
A catalogue record for
this book is available
from the British Library.

ISBN 0-7445-3639-1

# THINK OF AN EEL

Written by
## Karen Wallace

Illustrated by
## Mike Bostock

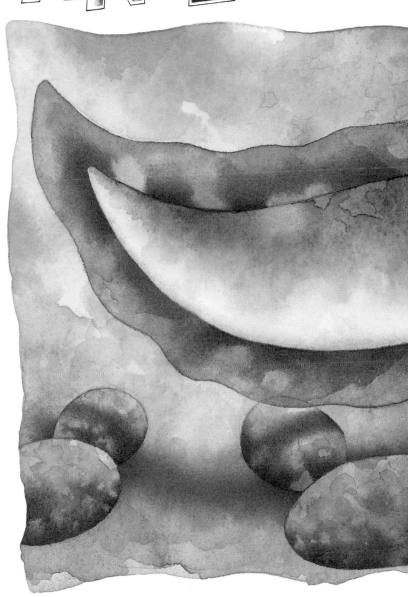

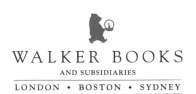

WALKER BOOKS
AND SUBSIDIARIES
LONDON · BOSTON · SYDNEY

Think of an eel.

He swims like a fish.

He slides like a snake.

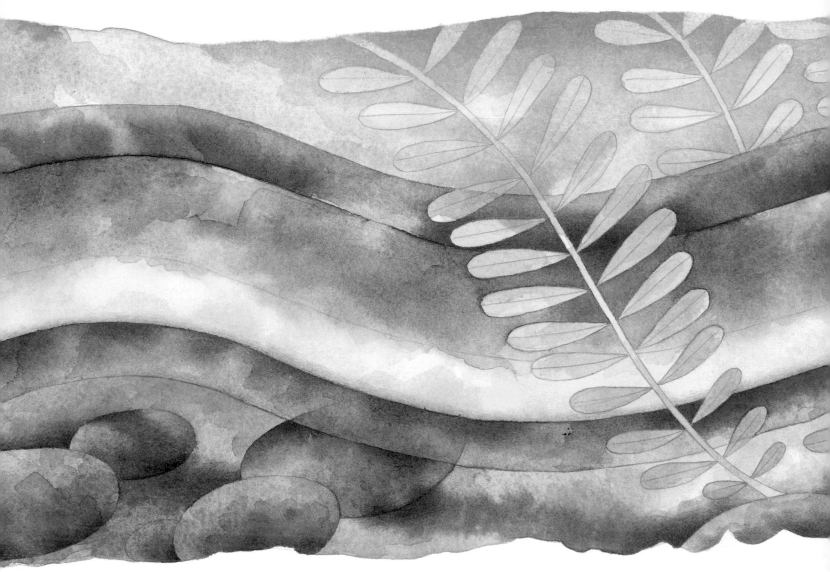

There's a warm, weedy sea
to the south of Bermuda.
It's called the Sargasso.
No wind ever blows there,
no sailing ships sail there.
For thousands of years there
a secret lay hidden:
this salt, soupy sea
is where eels are born.
Deep down where it's blackest,
eel egg becomes eel.
He looks like a willow leaf,
clear as a crystal.

Baby eels are born in early spring.
A real one is only

about this big.

His fierce jutting mouth
has teeth like a sawblade.

He eats like a horse and
swims up through the water.

Young eels from the Sargasso travel either to Europe or to America — whichever

*their parents did before them.*

Imagine this eel-leaf
and millions just like him
swimming on waves
across the wide sea.
Some are unlucky.
The seagulls are waiting.
Beaks snap like scissors
through wriggling water.

 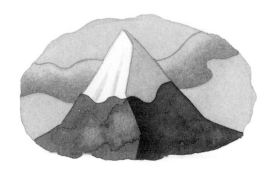

Eel swims for three years
till he reaches the shore

but the river's too cold, there's
still snow on the mountains.

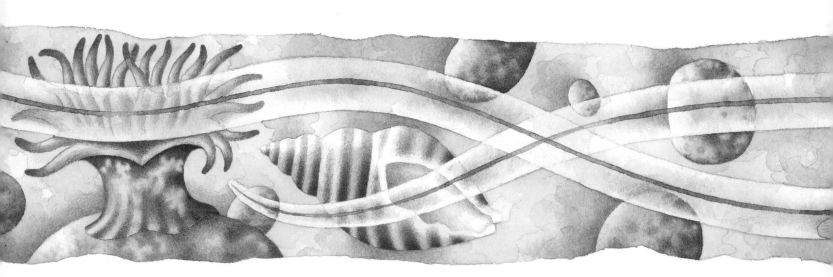

Eels arrive in Europe around Christmas time. They wait offshore

So he waits in the water,
turns into an elver.

Now he looks like a shoelace
made out of glass.

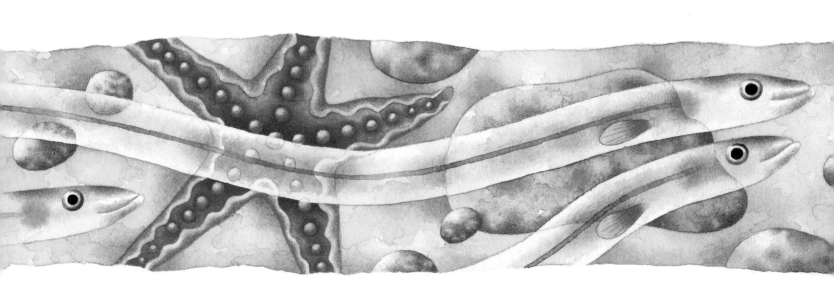

*until spring, and as they wait they turn into elvers.*

When spring
warms the shoreline,
the smell of fresh water
excites the glass elver.
Into the river
he swims like a mad thing.
He wriggles up rapids,
climbs rocks
around waterfalls.
River banks guide him.
Nothing will stop him.

*Eels navigate by instinct.*

They always seem to know where they are going.

Around a drowned oak stump,
through twisting green weeds,
a mudhole is hidden.

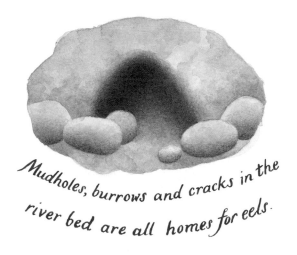

Mudholes, burrows and cracks in the
river bed are all homes for eels.

Eel knows without thinking
it's what he's been seeking.
He slips through the ooze.
This hole is his home.

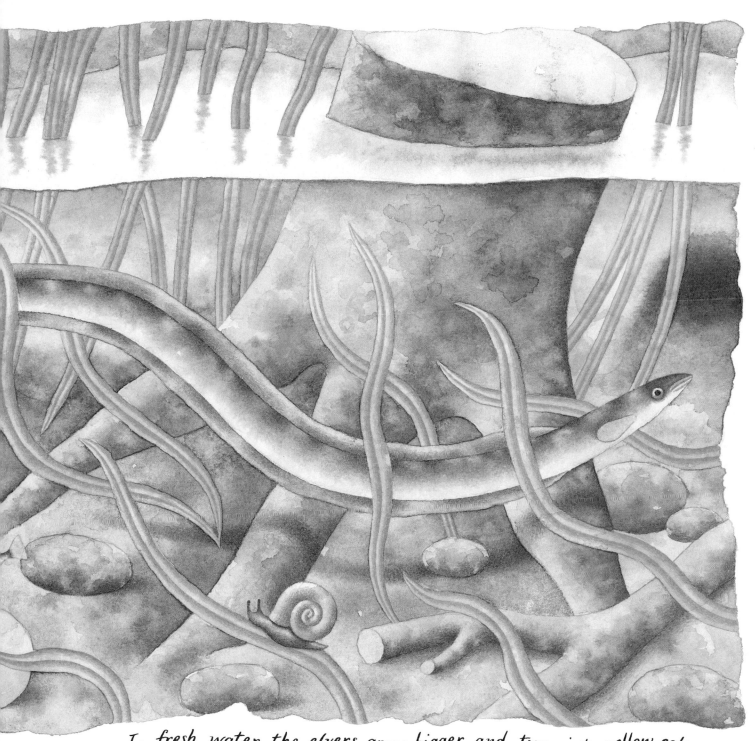

In fresh water, the elvers grow bigger and turn into yellow eels.

Think of an eel.
After years in the river
he's slit-eyed and slimy
and thick like a snake.
He gulps stickleback eggs,
eats shrimps and small fishes.

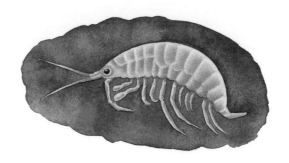

*shrimp*

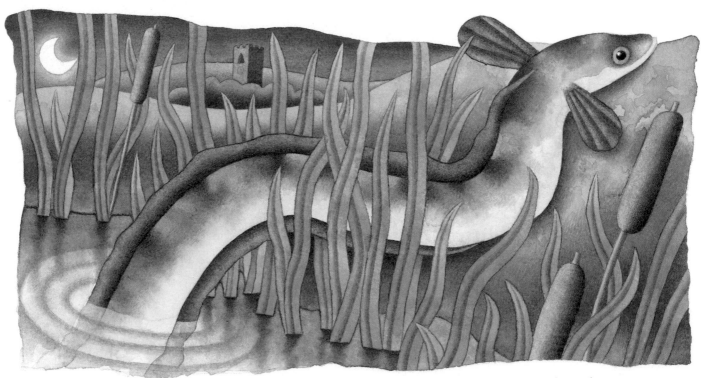

*Eels feed mostly at night.*

If the river is empty
he swims from the mudhole,
slips through the grass
to steal snails from the pond.

pond snail

An eel can live out of water for two days
or longer, if the ground is wet, breathing through its slimy skin.

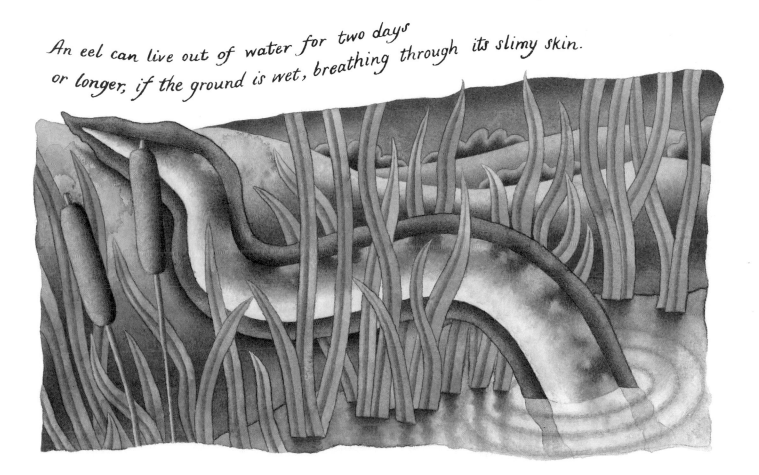

One day eel stops eating.
His stomach is shrinking.
His long winding body
turns silver and black.
Eyes like blackcurrants
bulge into headlamps.
Now for the last time
eel slides from the mudhole.
His years in the river
are over for ever.

*Silver eels usually leave the river in September or October.*

Silver eel waits

for a night that is moonless,

when the rain from the mountains

has flooded the stream.

While they're waiting for a dark night, they sometimes get tangled up in a ball.

Then he slips
down the river, down to
the seashore. The time has arrived
for his long journey home.

For eighty days
silver eel swims through the ocean,
squirms like a secret
from seabird and sailor.

There are millions just like him,

deep down in the water,

swimming silently back

to the Sargasso Sea.

*big eyes for seeing in the dark*

There's eel-tomb and eel-cradle
in the weedy Sargasso.
After eighty days' swimming,
not eating, not sleeping,
eel's long, winding body
is worn out and wasted.
He spills the new life
carried deep in his belly,
then sinks through the sea
like a used silver wrapper.

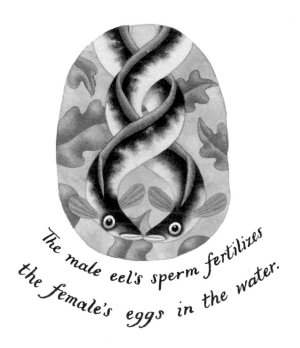

The male eel's sperm fertilizes the female's eggs in the water.

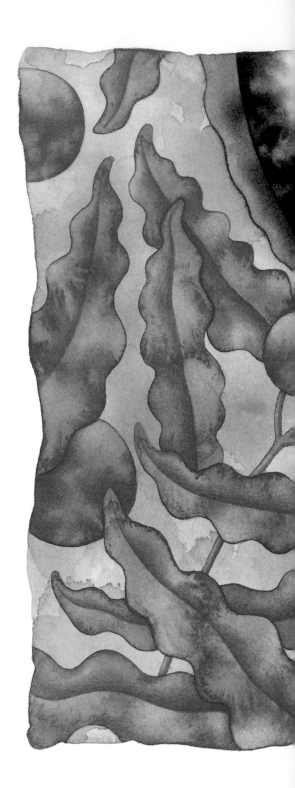

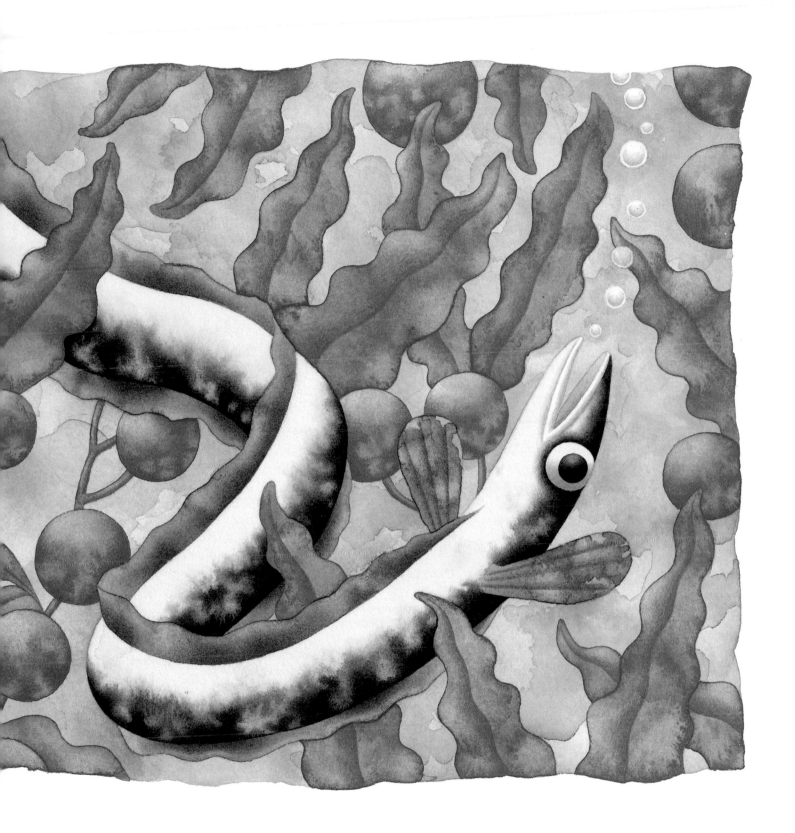

Deep down where it's blackest,
eel egg becomes eel.
He looks like a willow leaf,
clear as a crystal.
His fierce jutting mouth
has teeth like a sawblade.
He eats like a horse and
swims up through the water.

Imagine this eel-leaf
and millions just like him
swimming on waves
across the wide sea…

## Index

Look up the pages to find
out about all these eel things. Don't
forget to look at both kinds of words:
this kind *and this kind*.

# MORE WALKER PAPERBACKS
## For You to Enjoy

"These books fulfil all the requirements of a factual picture book, but also supply that imaginative element." *The Independent on Sunday*

"Beautifully illustrated books, written with style and humour."
*The Times Educational Supplement*

### ALL PIGS ARE BEAUTIFUL
by Dick-King Smith/Anita Jeram
0-7445-3635-9

### CATERPILLAR CATERPILLAR
by Vivian French/Charlotte Voake
0-7445-3636-7

### THINK OF A BEAVER
by Karen Wallace/Mick Manning
0-7445-3638-3

### THINK OF AN EEL
by Karen Wallace/Mike Bostock
(Winner of the Times Educational Supplement Junior Information
Book Award and the Kurt Maschler Award)
0-7445-3639-1

### WHAT IS A WALL, AFTER ALL?
by Judy Allen/Alan Baron
0-7445-3640-5

### I LIKE MONKEYS BECAUSE...
by Peter Hansard/Patricia Casey
0-7445-3646-4

### A FIELD FULL OF HORSES
by Peter Hansard/Kenneth Lilly
0-7445-3645-6

### A PIECE OF STRING IS A WONDERFUL THING
by Judy Hindley/Margaret Chamberlain
0-7445-3637-5

£4.99 each